MY PET
A PHOTOLOG BOOK

Created by Janet Horowitz
and Kathy Faggella

Illustrated by Steve Jenkins

Stewart, Tabori & Chang
New York

Your pet is a very important part of your life. You know that the world is full of people with pets, and that pets can come in all varieties. Yet, for you, your pet is that one special creature that you care for and is there for you to love. So, wouldn't it be nice to have a place to record the many things you'd like to remember about your pet? Wouldn't it be fun to take photos and share them with your family and friends?

You can! Right in this book. Here is the place for you to create a book all about your own special pet. With this book, a camera, film, and a little time spent with your pet, you can learn a lot about your pet and about yourself as well. You can be a photographer, reporter, and writer of your own PhotoLog book about you and your pet.

Uses for your **My Pet** book:

• Use **My Pet** as a fun way to discover more about your pet. As you play with and photograph your pet, you might see habits and instincts that you never noticed before. Record these new discoveries in this book.

• Use **My Pet** to help you understand the needs of your pet.

• Use **My Pet** as a book to share with family, friends, and classmates. Compare your pet's habits and reactions with those of your friend's pets. Be proud of and enjoy your pet's uniqueness.

• Use **My Pet** to record the significant events in your pet's life that you share together.

• Use **My Pet** as a treasured memory book, to help you remember the fun times you spend together.

Some hints to help you complete your book:

1. Take photos.
Be prepared to take photos of your pet that will fit the photo captions. One roll of 24-print film will be enough for this book. Try and take photos that show your pet behaving as naturally as possible.

2. Observe your pet.
In between the picture taking, notice what your pet does. Observe your pet's behavior in different situations. Watch how other family members and friends relate to your pet. Note how your pet acts with you.

3. Fill in this book.
When your pictures are ready, decide which ones would best fit the photo captions and pages of this book. Then complete the pages. Most answers can be found by watching and observing, others from talking with your friends and family. Follow the order in this book, or skip around, whatever makes you feel comfortable.
You do not have to fill in everything.
And remember, have fun!

My pet is a [kind]:

- ❑ dog
- ❑ bird
- ❑ reptile
- ❑ monkey
- ❑ rodent
- ❑ cat
- ❑ fish
- ❑ amphibian
- ❑ rock
- ❑ guinea pig
- ❑ A (visiting only) wild animal

I chose this particular pet because _____

_____ .

MY PET

My pet's full name is _____.

This name was chosen because _____.

Other names my pet is often called are _____

_____.

My full name is _____.

This name was chosen for me by _____

_____.

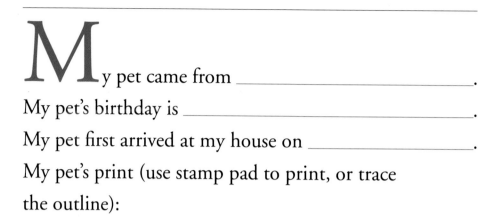

My pet came from _____.

My pet's birthday is _____.

My pet first arrived at my house on _____.

My pet's print (use stamp pad to print, or trace the outline):

MY PET AS A BABY

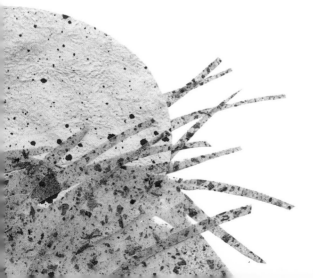

Long ago, most pet's ancestors probably lived in the wild. Draw a line between a family pet and its wild relative, and circle the pair that most resembles your pet:

puppy	lion
salamander	shark
canary bird	wolf
kitten	rat
turtle	eagle
goldfish	alligator
gerbil	giant tortoise

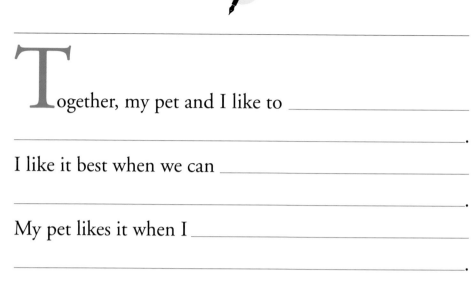

Together, my pet and I like to _____
_____.

I like it best when we can _____
_____.

My pet likes it when I _____
_____.

M y pet's favorite food is _____.

My pet's favorite snack treat is _____.

My pet's food:

❏ smells awful ❏ is people food ❏ is alive

❏ smells delicious ❏ is a special diet ❏ _____

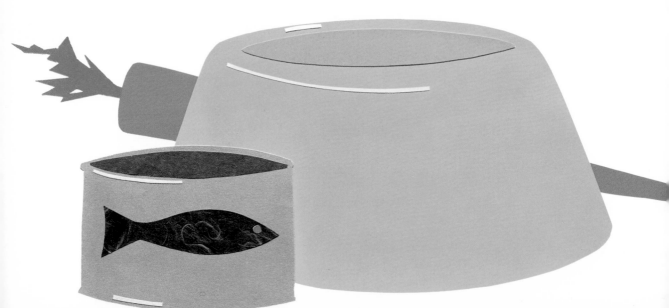

MY PET'S FOOD

The person who is supposed to feed my pet is

_____.

The person who usually feeds my pet is _____.

My pet's usual place to eat is _____.

The place my pet is not allowed to eat is _____

_____.

My pet's eating schedule is:

❏ once a day   ❏ once a week

❏ twice a day   ❏ all the time

❏ three times a day   ❏ other _____

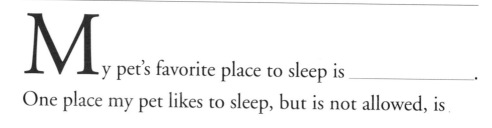

M

y pet's favorite place to sleep is _____.
One place my pet likes to sleep, but is not allowed, is _____
_____.

Draw in the hours your pet likes to sleep:

While I am asleep, by pet is _____.

Things my pet and I need to be comfortable and happy are [check]:

MY PET		ME
❏	house	❏
❏	food	❏
❏	clothes	❏
❏	toys	❏
❏	food dish	❏
❏	leash	❏
❏	bed	❏
❏	carrying case	❏
❏	ID tags	❏

Something special my pet can do is _____.

My pet learned how to do this from _____.

I would like to have my pet:

- ❏ learn how to "play dead"
- ❏ catch a frisbee
- ❏ become a famous movie star
- ❏ frighten an intruder
- ❏ clean up after him/herself
- ❏ jump through a hoop
- ❏ have its face on pet products
- ❏ shake hello

My pet gets dirty when _____.

The way my pet keeps clean is _____.

I help my pet keep clean by _____.

Places my pet has used as a bathroom are [check]:

❑ entire outdoor world   ❑ sand

❑ flower garden   ❑ furniture in my house

❑ newspaper   ❑ a special box

❑ floors in my house   ❑ cage

❑ other

Put an X on the ones that shouldn't be used.

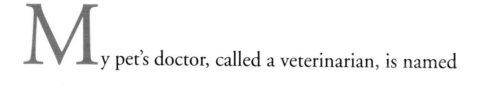

My pet's doctor, called a veterinarian, is named

_____ .

The doctor thinks my pet is _____ .

Here is my pet's doctor's autograph:

He/she became an animal doctor because _____

_____ .

The telephone number to call if my pet is sick is

_____ .

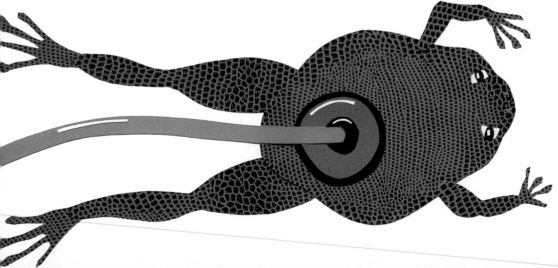

When I'm busy or at school, I think my pet is usually:

- ❏ getting into mischief
- ❏ waiting for me
- ❏ playing with toys
- ❏ _____

- ❏ hiding
- ❏ exercising
- ❏ sleeping

When I come home, my pet:

- ❏ is happy to see me
- ❏ is hiding
- ❏ begs for a walk
- ❏ wants to play
- ❏ _____

- ❏ gives me a kiss
- ❏ is usually asleep
- ❏ ignores me
- ❏ makes a funny sound

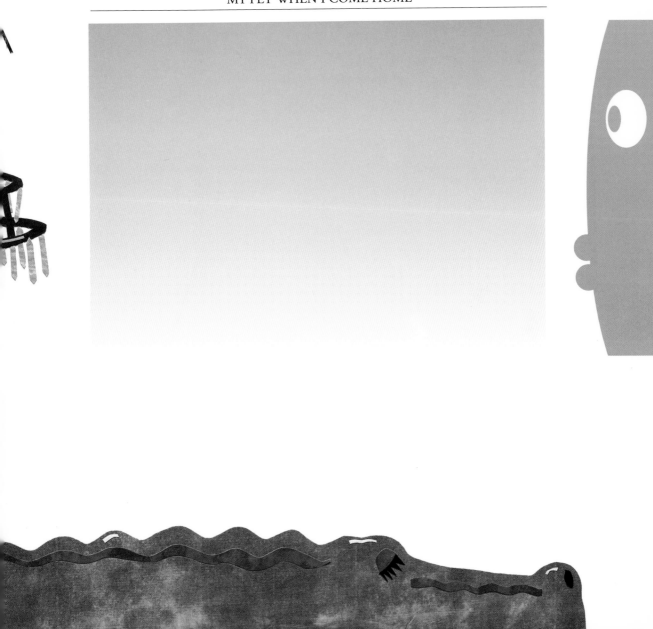

My pet's friends are _____
_____.

When they are together, they like to _____
_____.

My pet would like to play with _____
_____.

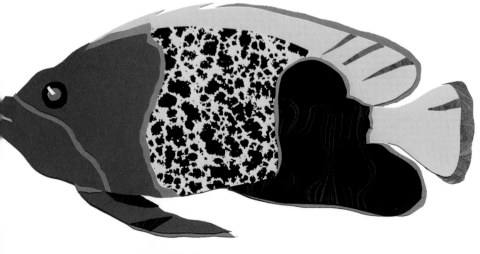

Friends of mine who like my pet are _____
_____.

Friends of mine who do not like my pet are _____
_____

My friends describe my pet as _____.

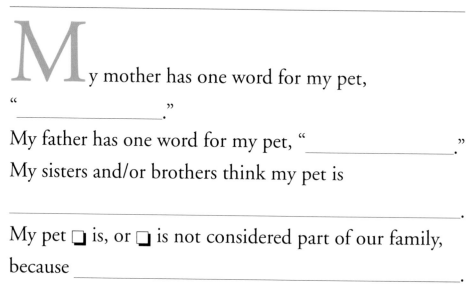

My mother has one word for my pet,
"_____."
My father has one word for my pet, "_____."
My sisters and/or brothers think my pet is

_____.

My pet ❑ is, or ❑ is not considered part of our family,
because _____.

A FAMILY PICTURE

My pet goes out [check]:

☐ in a box/cage ☐ on a leash

☐ in my pocket ☐ in my arms

☐ in my backpack ☐ _____

Where we go:

☐ to the vet ☐ to the country

☐ to school ☐ for a walk

☐ through the city ☐ to visit friends

☐ on a ride ☐ _____

Circle the ones your pet likes and put an X on the ones your pet dislikes.

The scariest thing that ever happened to my pet was

_____.

The funniest thing that I still laugh about is _____

_____.

My pet ☐ is, or ☐ is not a "party animal" because

_____.

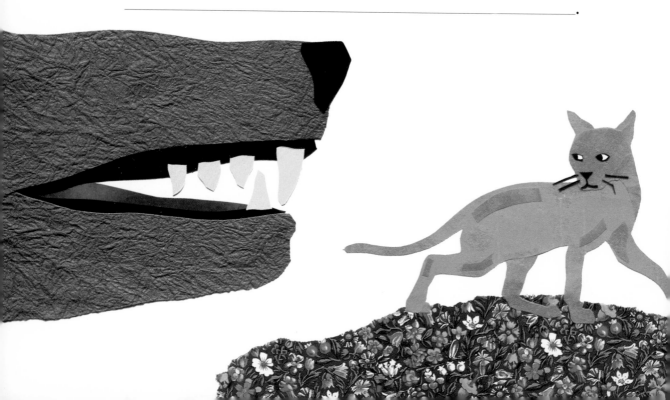

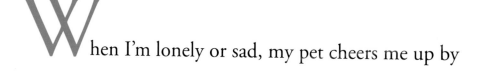

When I'm lonely or sad, my pet cheers me up by
_____.

My pet gets attention by _____.

I can tell when my pet is:

❑ happy, because _____.

❑ sad, because _____.

❑ hungry, because _____.

❑ ill, because _____.

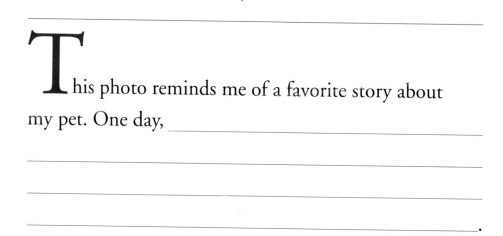

This photo reminds me of a favorite story about my pet. One day, _____

_____
_____
_____
_____ .

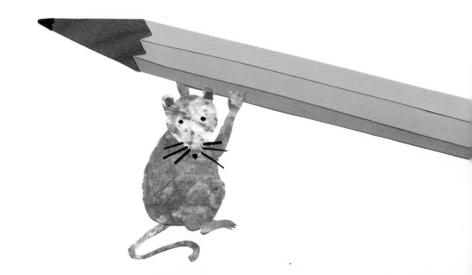

The important dates to remember in my pet's life are:

- ❏ birthday _____.
- ❏ when housebroken _____.
- ❏ first went up and down stairs _____.
- ❏ first new teeth _____.
- ❏ first bath _____.
- ❏ other _____

Paste in certificates here:

AN IMPORTANT DAY

Design by Jenkins & Page, New York, NY.
Composed in-house in Adobe Garamond with QuarkXpress 3.0.
Output by The Sarabande Press, New York, NY.
Printed and bound by Toppan Printing Company, Ltd., Singapore.